S0-BNR-852

STAGE 1

What Makes a Shadow?

REVISED EDITION

By Clyde Robert Bulla

Illustrated by June Otani

SOUTHERN LEHIGH PUBLIC LIBRARY

HarperCollinsPublishers

The *Let's-Read-and-Find-Out Science* book series was originated by Dr. Franklyn M. Branley, Astronomer Emeritus and former Chairman of the American Museum–Hayden Planetarium, and was formerly co-edited by him and Dr. Roma Gans, Professor Emeritus of Childhood Education, Teachers College, Columbia University. Text and illustrations for each of the books in the series are checked for accuracy by an expert in the relevant field. For a complete catalog of Let's-Read-and-Find-Out Science books, write to HarperCollins Children's Books, 10 East 53rd Street, New York, NY 10022.

Let's Read-and-Find-Out Science is a registered trademark of HarperCollins Publishers.

What Makes a Shadow?

Text copyright © 1962, 1994 by Clyde Robert Bulla
Illustrations copyright © 1994 by June Otani
All rights reserved. No part of this book may be used or reproduced in any manner whatsoever without written permission except in the case of brief quotations embodied in critical articles and reviews. Printed in the United States of America. For information address HarperCollins Children's Books, a division of HarperCollins Publishers, 10 East 53rd Street, New York, NY 10022.
1 2 3 4 5 6 7 8 9 10 ❖
Revised Edition

Library of Congress Cataloging-in-Publication Data
Bulla, Clyde Robert.
    What makes a shadow? / by Clyde Robert Bulla ; illustrated by June Otani. — Rev. ed.
        p.   cm. — (Let's-read-and-find-out science. Stage 1)
    Summary: A simple explanation of how a shadow is formed.
    ISBN 0-06-022915-2. — ISBN 0-06-022916-0 (lib. bdg.) — ISBN 0-06-445118-6 (pbk.)
    1. Shades and shadows—Juvenile literature.   [1. Shadows.]
I. Otani, June, ill.   II. Title.   III. Series.
QC381.6.B84   1994   92-36350
535.4—dc20   CIP
                                                                              AC

What Makes a Shadow?

The sun is shining. It shines on the trees and the sidewalk. It shines on your house.
   It shines on you, too.

When the sun is in front of you, look behind you. You can see your shadow. When you move, your shadow moves. When you run, your shadow runs. But you can never catch it.

What makes the shadow? Where does it come from?

The sun is very bright. It shines on the house. It shines on the trees. It shines on you. But the sun does not shine *through* you.

There is a dark place behind you where the sun does not shine. The darkness is your shadow.

Look for more shadows.

A tree has a shadow. The shade of the tree is the shadow of the tree.

A **house** has a shadow.

The sun shines on one side of the house. There is a shadow on the other side.

Animals have shadows.

So do cars.

14

Airplanes have shadows. Watch as an airplane flies over your head. You may see its shadow on the ground.

A cloud has a shadow.

Sometimes the sky is dark with clouds. The sun cannot shine through them. The shadows of the clouds fall on the earth. The shadows make the day dark. We say, "This is a cloudy day."

Some shadows are darker than others. Hold a paper towel so the sun shines on it. The paper towel makes a shadow on the ground. The shadow is not dark because some of the sunlight shines through.

Hold a book so the sun shines on it. The book makes a
shadow on the ground. It makes a dark shadow because
no sunlight shines through.

Watch the sun go down.

Watch the night come.

Night is a shadow.

The sun shines on one side of the earth. The other side is
in shadow. The shadow makes the night.

Inside the house at night you can see more shadows. Hold
your hand between a lamp and the wall. You will see the
shadow of your hand on the wall.

Do you know how to make a big shadow?
Hold your hand close to the lamp, but not too close. The light
bulb may be hot! The shadow is big because your hand shuts
out so much of the light. This makes more darkness on the wall.

Move your hand away from the light. Move it farther and farther away. Now the shadow on the wall gets smaller and smaller and smaller. It is smaller because your hand does not shut out so much light. There is less darkness on the wall.

You can have fun with shadows. Hold your hands between
the light and the wall and make shadow pictures. You can make a
duck. Or a dog. Or a rabbit.

You can make shadow pictures little or big. You can move
your hands to make the pictures move.

There are other shadow pictures you can make. Here are some.

Look for shadows. How many can you find?

When you find shadows, see if you can discover what makes each one.

DATE DUE

ER
535.4
Bul

Bulla, Clyde Robert
What makes a shadow?

Southern Lehigh Public Library
3200 Preston Lane
P.O. Box 279
Center Valley, PA. 18034